Carl C. Plehn

Finances of the United States in the Spanish War

Carl C. Plehn

Finances of the United States in the Spanish War

ISBN/EAN: 9783337010577

Printed in Europe, USA, Canada, Australia, Japan

Cover: Foto ©Suzi / pixelio.de

More available books at **www.hansebooks.com**

UNIVERSITY OF CALIFORNIA

———

Finances of the United States in the Spanish War

THREE LECTURES

BY

CARL C. PLEHN

———

[Reprinted from THE UNIVERSITY CHRONICLE, Vol. I, No. 5]

———

BERKELEY
THE UNIVERSITY PRESS
1898

FINANCES OF THE UNITED STATES
IN THE SPANISH WAR.*

By CARL C. PLEHN.

I.—RAISING THE FUNDS.

There were many things connected with the management of the war with Spain which reflected great credit on the government of the United States. Not less creditable than the exploits of our army and navy was the general financial administration of the war. The vast sums requisite were obtained promptly and without serious disturbance of the money market or of the general level of prices. We floated a war loan with the utmost ease at a rate of interest lower than that which any nation has ever before paid during war times; and for the first time in our history the credit of the country was so used that it grew stronger rather than weaker from its use.

While there are many features of the war revenue bill itself which are open to criticism, especially in that part which deals with taxation, yet the general plan for the fiscal administration of the war is in almost exact accord with the accepted principles of Public Finance. In this respect it forms a striking contrast to the fiscal management of any other war by the United States.

---

*Three lectures delivered before the students in History and Political Science, September 22 and 29, and October 6, 1898.

Before beginning to study the actual administration of our finances in the recent war it will be conducive to clearness if we recall, briefly, what is generally considered to be the sound method for the fiscal administration of a war. A serious war usually imposes a sudden, new burden upon the treasury, the exact, or even the approximate, size of which it is not possible to estimate at the outset. Many of the expenses of war belong to that class which financiers call "extra-ordinary" to distinguish them from the usual or current expenses of the government. The amount by which the ordinary expenses are increased in time of war depends upon many circumstances. Obviously, the chief factor is the size of the forces engaged and the duration of the struggle. Naturally, the chastisement of a few dozen hostile Indian braves in the immediate vicinity of the regular army posts involves practically no "extra-ordinary" expenses. Allowance is usually made in the ordinary budget for the expenses a war of that kind would occasion. But many circumstances less obvious than the size of the forces engaged enter into the determination of the amount of the "extra-ordinary" expenditures. Thus, for example, a naval war, unless it happens to become the occasion for the purchase of new ships, involves comparatively little addition to the ordinary expenses of maintaining the navy. A country which has a large standing army incurs relatively less "extra-ordinary" expense when engaging in war than a country which like ours has only a small regular army. For very obvious reasons, practically all the expenses of this war except so far as the regular navy was engaged were among the "extra-ordinary" ones, and had to be met by the treasury by means of distinct additions to our ordinary revenues.

The ordinary expenses being provided for by the regular budget the financier's whole concern in time of war is the provision of the "extra-ordinary" funds. If the operations of the war are likely to interfere with the ordinary revenues he must furthermore be prepared to treat a part of the ordinary expenses as "extra-ordinary," at least to the extent of furnishing new means to meet them. It is not often possible, and still less often expedient to curtail the ordinary expenditures in any way for the purpose of saving money to meet the new expenses. How to increase the receipts of the treasury by an amount sufficient to ensure the efficient conduct of the war, without too serious disturbance of the industries and commerce of the people, upon which all the revenues depend, is the problem for the finance minister to solve. The "extra-ordinary" demands come thick and fast, especially at the beginning of the war and they must be met and met at once. The amount which may be needed at any given time is not ascertainable. But in spite of that, sufficient funds must always be on hand. Upon this more than upon any other one thing depends the fate of war. The war financier can never plead that he has no funds, nor can he ask for time in which to collect. He must have the money when it is wanted and in the amounts required. No degree of skill on the part of officers or bravery on the part of the men, no degree of self-sacrifice at the front can compensate for failure on the part of the financier to provide the ways and means. His powers are, therefore, of the greatest and most unusual.

Possibly the most natural source to turn to in time of war for the increased revenues needed is the existing system of taxes. At first thought it might seem proper to attempt to obtain new income by raising the rates of the old taxes. To some extent this is possible. In every well-arranged tax-system there should be some taxes which can be made to yield an increased revenue by simply raising the rates. One of the chief reasons for the establishment and the retention of the British "property and income tax," for example, is found in the elasticity of the returns. But not all taxes can be treated in this way. Sometimes an increase in the rate of taxation will disturb industry and commerce and do a greater injury to the welfare of the people than is received from the damages of war. Again an increase in the rates of certain taxes will diminish the revenue or even destroy it entirely. In not a few taxes the only way to increase the revenue is to lower the rates. This is the case with most protective duties. Any change in the rate of such taxes is bound to affect industry and commerce, and to affect them unfavorably in the first instance, whatever the subsequent effect may be. A war brings perplexities enough to business without the creation of artificial ones, and the financier should not interfere with these taxes. It added not a little to the perplexities and dangers of the civil war that the industry and commerce of the people were repeatedly disturbed during the war by changes in the tariff as well as by the military and naval operations themselves. There are, therefore, but a limited number of old taxes from which any aid can be sought. In our own country owing to our one-sided system of taxation, the number of them is very small indeed. The financier must look elsewhere for his new revenues.

The next resource, naturally, is new taxes. But the establishment of new taxes or even the restoration of old taxes not in use at the time of the war is a matter requiring considerable time. Even if it were an easy matter to decide upon the best form of taxation and to get the necessary authority from the legislative branch of the government, the organization of the new administrative forces for the collection of the taxes is a matter requiring time. No new system of taxation reaches its normal revenue-yielding powers within many months of its enactment. If the taxes are entirely new the time required is longer. But even if they are more or less familiar to the people from use on some previous occasion, a considerable lapse of time must intervene between the beginning of war and the receipt of sufficient new revenues to meet any considerable part of its expenses. Furthermore, the expenses of war are now so enormous that any system of taxation which raised, or attempted to raise, the entire amount needed during the probable duration of the war would be so burdensome as to crush the people. It is therefore extremely unwise, and practically impossible, to attempt to raise the entire cost of the war by immediate taxation. The only other resource is borrowing.

The use of the public credit, in time of war, is attended by many special difficulties. The outcome of war is always more or less uncertain. Even if defeat would not entirely cripple the nation's resources and render the repayment of the loan uncertain, or affect the payment of interest, yet there are many considerations which make the lender hesitate. The fact that the duration of the war, the extent to which other nations may become involved, and many similar considerations affecting the size of the total demand upon the public credit are unknown, vastly increases the difficulty of placing a loan on favorable terms. But on that very account it is particularly necessary for the successful administration of the war that everything should be done to strengthen and preserve the nation's credit. There may come a time in the progress of the war when the only source from which any funds can be had is the money market. If, therefore, the financier has done anything to weaken the nation's credit at the beginning of the war he is apt to be helpless at the close. Credit tends to weaken as debt increases.

It is for this reason that resort is. usually had in early war-borrowings to the simplest and most primitve method of debt-making: namely, that which provides revenues for the payment of the interest and the repayment of the principal at the very time the debt is contracted. The creditor sees in the new funds flowing into the treasury the security for his advances, and the guarantee of good faith on the part of the government. So long as every new loan is accompanied by new taxes from which its cost can be met the public credit is practically secure. But if on the other hand the government neglect this precaution during the first stages of the war, any attempt to resort to it at a later stage is apt to be regarded as the desperate device of unsound financial management and the presage of coming bankruptcy.

Public credit is a plant of slow growth and extremely tender. It withers in a day before a breath of doubt.

Inasmuch as a successful outcome cannot be hoped for in modern warfare without the funds obtainable solely by public borrowing, and the necessity for loans increases the longer the war continues, it behooves the modern war financier to guard the nation's credit as his most precious treasure. No sacrifice is too great which will strengthen it and preserve it intact for the later stages of the war.

Such, stated in a form almost too condensed for perfect clearness, are the principles which should guide the *fiscus* in time of war. No better illustration of the application of these principles can be found in history than is afforded by our recent war.

The situation, as it confronted Secretary Gage when the news of the destruction of the Maine reached Washington, may be summarised somewhat as follows: The Treasury had a balance on hand of about $225,000,000. But, as we shall see in a moment, only about $25,000,000 of this was really available for immediate use in the prosecution of the war. The ordinary expenditures of the government, outside of those for the postal system, which is nearly self-supporting, amounted in round numbers to $350,000,000 per annum. For the first time in many months these expenses were being nearly met by the revenues. Indeed it was estimated that at the ordinary rate of expenditures there might be a slight surplus at the end of the year. The tariff was expected to yield about $200,000,000, the internal revenue taxes about $165,000,000, and there were about $25,000,000 to be expected from miscellaneous sources.

The larger part of the income, however, came from taxes which could not well be tampered with. The tariff had been so long a subject of controversy, that there was little desire to alter its recent settlement. For reasons already made clear there were many parts of the tariff which could not well be changed. Except in a very few instances the income to be obtained from it would not be increased by raising the rates. In the great majority of instances to raise the rates would have been to lessen the receipts, while to lower those rates for the purpose of increasing the income by allowing larger importations would have been to remove the protection afforded by them. This was contrary to the avowed policy of the administration. It would, moreover, have served to disturb industry and to preplex its leaders at a time already sufficiently disquieting, and might have proved but an aggravation of the disturbance caused by the war. The great body of the customs rates, of which there are thousands on our tariff schedules, are not productive of much revenue and are not intended to be. They are there to restrict importations. These certainly could not well be changed. Of the bare dozen or so of articles of importation which do yield a revenue, sugar, one of the most important, was likely to be interfered with by the war. At the existing rates, sugar imported should yield a revenue of about $80,000,000 a year, but at least half of the importation was jeopardized by the war itself and it would have been highly impolitic to have changed the rate at this time. Iron, which was once a source of considerable revenue, was, in consequence of the changes which have taken place in that industry, and of the protective features of the customs law, not available to provide new revenues, as the importations are at best small. Cotton goods, the tax upon which yields considerable revenue, were protected; so were manufactures of hemp, flax and jute, of leather and of wool. Drugs, medicines, and chemicals were already taxed up to the limit of productiveness from a revenue point of view. In short there were but four important articles imported which might be used to yield additional revenue. These were hides and skins, raw silk, and tea and coffee. To tax hides and skins, and raw silk would, probably, under the prevailing theory of "compensatory" duties, have involved an increase in the rates on the products manufactured from them, to maintain the same degree of protection that those products now enjoy. That would have reopened the whole tariff controversy and have rendered the outcome of the war-revenue measure extremely doubtful. Clearly it were wisest, considering how recently the tariff issue had been temporarily settled, to leave them alone. As a matter of fact, then, there are only two articles in the whole list of importations which might be considered by the Secretary of the Treasury in his search for new income. These were tea and coffee, which might, perhaps, have been made to yield together nearly $80,000,000 additional revenue. That was approximately all that could be expected from the tariff.

In the war revenue bill as presented to the House of Representatives by the Committee on Ways and Means, of which Mr. Dingley was chairman, there was no suggestion of using the tariff in any way for obtaining additional revenue. It was not until the very end of the long discussion of the measure in the Senate that it was proposed to put a duty of 10 cents a pound on tea. That measure passed the Senate and was accepted by the conference between the two Houses and by the House of Representatives without any public discussion as to its merits. The reason for this duty, as for the omission of coffee from the list, is therefore not clear. The tax on tea is an important matter. The yield will be over $10,000,000 per annum. A similar tax on coffee, which would have been at the rate of 8.5 cents per pound, would have yielded about $70,000,000 more. It is, therefore, somewhat surprising that it should have attracted so little attention from the members of Congress.

Since the revenue from the tariff was not to be increased the only resource available was internal taxes. That these internal taxes should have taken the same general form as the taxes used during the civil war, and consequently more or less familiar to people and officers, was but natural. Under the stress of war it is unwise to attempt to organize entirely new taxes, such, for example, as an income tax. Though an income tax had been used during the civil war, that form of taxation was under the shadow of an adverse decision from the Supreme Court. Even if an income tax law which would have been constitutional, according to the recent decision of the court, could have been drawn, it is doubtful whether it could have been made productive within any reasonable period of time. Recourse might have been had to direct taxes apportioned among the States according to population. These taxes could then have been raised in any manner which the State authorities chose. But there are two fatal objections to this plan. The apportionment of taxes according to population is fundamentally unjust and unequal. What it amounts to practically is a graduated poll tax. The different commonwealths vary so in wealth *per capita* that any *per capita* tax, however raised, would be unfair. Although the census estimate of wealth in 1890 was anything but satisfactory, yet the method used in that estimate was uniform throughout the country; and such differences as that between South Carolina, with about $350 *per capita*, and Nevada, with $4,000 *per capita*, show how utterly inadequate the constitutional method of raising direct taxes has become. Then again, the method of taxation by which most of the States raise their revenues, and which they would probably follow in raising their share of any apportioned taxes, is the worst in use in any civilized country and the injustice of the apportionment would have been enormously increased by the injustice in collection. The second objection to this method of raising direct taxes prescribed by the constitution is that it takes an inordinate length of time, and war taxes should begin to yield a revenue as early as possible.

The only available plan was, therefore, to seek additional revenue from the existing, indirect, internal taxes, the excises or, as we call them, the "internal revenue taxes, and to supplement these still further by new taxes of the same sort. The critical examination of the war revenue-bill forms the subject of the second of these lectures, so I must content myself here with the brief statement that the government resorted at this critical period to increased rates on some of the existing internal revenue taxes and to certain of the taxes used during the Civil War. Briefly summarized the revenue bill nearly doubled the existing rate of taxation upon beer and other similar fermented liquors; it imposed special taxes on bankers, brokers, pawn-brokers, theatres, circuses, and other shows, bowling-alleys and billiard rooms; it raised the rates on tobacco of all kinds; and placed stamp taxes on stocks and bonds, commercial papers, legal documents, checks and drafts, proprietary medicines, toilet articles, bills of lading, insurance policies, and a number of other things. Special direct taxes were imposed on the oil-trust and the sugar-trust; and on legacies and distributive shares of personal property.

As the war revenue bill passed the House its probable yield was variously estimated at from $90,000,000 to $105,000,000 per annum, the former being the better esti-mate. As amended in the Senate and finally adopted, it promised to yield at least $150,000,000 per annum. The actual yield in addition to the regular revenue during the first month was about $13,000,000 which speaks well for the probable accuracy of this estimate. But the expenses of war during the first few months, if not for a long time after that, would be, it was estimated, at least double that sum and possibly more. Therefore, unless the Treasury had a considerable balance on hand, there would have been no possibility of conducting the war at all without immediate loans. The balance in the Treasury at the outbreak of the war was $225,000,000. Upon this were a number of claims, some of which, however, were not immediate. $100,000,000, known as the gold reserve, had to be held for the preserva-tion of the parity of all parts of the circulation and the avoidance of general financial ruin. Then there were $13,000,000 of fractional silver and minor coins, a large part of which was worn and unavailable, while the rest was needed for currency purposes throughout the country. $14,000,000 had been received from the sale of the Pacific Railroads; but although this sum was temporarily available it would, if it were spent, be necessary to raise an equivalent amount before January first to meet the Pacific Railroad bonds which came due at that time. $33,000,000 were held in trust for the redemption of the notes of national banks which had failed or which were redeeming their circulation. A part of this was temporarily available but it would be necessary to replenish that fund at an early date if much were drawn from it. There were then, out of the $225,000,000, $160,000,000 of which a small part only was available and that but for a short time. Anything drawn upon that would have to be replaced by January first at latest. Of the $65,000,000 remaining $40,000,000 were necessary as the cash on hand for the ordinary operations of the government. That amount corresponds to the cash on hand which a merchant keeps in the till to make change or to meet small bills. This left but $25,000,000 for the initial expenses of the war which in our state of unpreparedness would naturally be above the average. This $25,000,000 was all the unencumbered money in the Treasury to meet the appropriation of $50,000,000 made by Congress before war was declared. It was clear that the Secretary of the Treasury could not provide the sinews of war without the power to borrow, both for a short time, to anticipate the revenues expected from the new taxes, and for a long time to enable him to support any naval and military operations which might become necessary, however extensive.

After much discussion and more or less unnecessary and dangerous delay, especially in the Senate, Congress authorized the borrowing, at the discretion of the administration, of not more than $100,000,000 at any one time on Treasury

certificates and of an amount not to exceed $400,000,000 on
10–20 bonds at three per cent. Nominally, therefore, the
Secretary of the Treasury had in his hands for the necessities of war during the first six months of its duration:

Surplus on hand	$ 25,000,000
War revenues	75,000,000
Temporary loans	100,000,000
Bonds	400,000,000
Total	$600,000,000

Practically, he was limited by the fact that all of this
money had not been appropriated and it would have been
folly to raise more than he had authority to spend.
Including the $50,000,000 appropriated before the war
broke out, the total war appropriations made by Congress
before it adjourned amounted in all to $361,788,095.11.
This sum covered the most generous estimates of the probable cost of the war. It is not possible at the present time
to obtain a complete estimate or a detailed account of
the actual expenses of the war. There is little doubt,
however, but that they will fall well within the appropriations. Even though the war is over, the "extra-ordinary"
demands on the Treasury will not cease for many months to
come. To the end of July, the expenses were about
$90,000,000; to the end of August about $115,000,000;
and for the six months they will probably be well within
$175,000,000, or within half of the appropriations. The
Treasury, meanwhile, has been in the receipt of about
$13,000,000 a month additional revenues, or about $75,000,-
000 for six months. It has also raised $200,000,000 by
the sale of 10–20 bonds at three per cent., a total of
$275,000,000, or nearly $100,000,000 in excess of the
probable actual expenditure for the six months. Although
the accumulation of this surplus will give rise to many
interesting problems in the future, it was not in any sense
an extravagant or useless piece of financiering. As was
stated in the beginning of this lecture, the Treasury must be
prepared to meet any demand that may arise, instantly and

amply. That is an imperative necessity. As the early close of the war could not have been foreseen, the fiscal preparations were necessarily liberal. Indeed the amplitude of the funds available was one of the most potent causes of the success of the war. The excess raised was not larger than was necessary to insure the instant readiness of the Treasury to meet all possible demands. Had the war continued and the demands equalled the appropriations, the Treasury would again have been obliged to use its power of borrowing which the fortunate termination of the war rendered unnecessary.

So far the general plan of the financial administration of the war corresponds to the ideal plan. It remains to see how the credit of the nation stood the strain. As a matter of fact we have come out of the war stronger in credit than we went in, and this in itself is a remarkable feat. Let us see how it was accomplished.

At the end of April, 1898, the interest bearing debt of the United States amounted in round numbers to $847,000,-000. $100,000,000 of this bore interest nominally at five per cent., the balance at four per cent. The four per cent. bonds payable in 1895 were quoted, when the plans were being made for placing the new loan, at 117¼. At that rate they would yield the investor three and one-quarter per cent. interest. There was, therefore, some surprise when it was proposed to place the new loan at three per cent. It was urged that nobody would buy the new bond at three per cent. when he could buy one of the old ones and get three and one-quarter per cent. Yet the outcome showed the wisdom of the move. The bonds were subscribed to seven times over and in a short time rose to a premium of 103 and 105. In fact the entire loan was easily placed on far better terms than any nation has ever before been able to obtain in time of war. This remarkable result was attained partly by reason of the fact that the loan was offered for popular subscriptions and the bonds were for small amounts, thus creating and reaching a new market among investors of small means. In part, too, it was due to the fact that the new bonds at par really formed a better basis for the national bank-note circulation than the old bonds at 117¼, and very much better than the old bonds at 123¼, the price which was reached before the new issue was completed. An investment by a national bank of $100,000 in the old bonds at 117¼ would yield a profit of $736.70 on the circulation, if interest is at six per cent.; while an investment of the same amount in the new bonds at par would yield a profit on the circulation of $1,302.02. The difference in favor of the new bonds was $565.32, or over half of one per cent. The advantage is still greater now as the old 4's are at 127½.* None of these influences, however, would have had any weight had it not been that new revenues sufficient to meet all debt charges and part of the war expenses had been provided.

Much interest centers around the successful attempt to make this a popular loan. Congress after much discussion, finally provided that these three per cent. bonds "redeemable in coin at the pleasure of the United States after ten years from the date of their issue and payable twenty years from

*COMPARATIVE ILLUSTRATION OF $100,000 INVESTMENT.

	3's OF 1908–18 AT PAR.		4's OF 1925 AT 117¼.	
Par value of bonds purchased	$100,000		$85,287.84	
Circulation	90,000		79,759.05	
Receipts:				
Interest on circulation, 6%	5,400		4,605.54	
Interest on bonds	3,000		3,411.51	
		$8,400		$8,017.05
Deductions:				
Tax on circulation	900		852.87	
Expenses	60.50		60.50	
Annual cost of redemption	137.48		137.48	
Sinking fund to liquidate premium	....		229.50	
		1,097.98		1,280.35
Net receipts	....	$7,302.02		$6,736.70
Receipts if capital had been invested, 6%	....	6,000		6,000
Profit on circulation	....	$1,302.02		$ 736.70

Advantage of 3's at par over the 4's at 117¼, $565.32 or .565%.

that date," should "be first offered at par as a popular loan
under such regulations, prescribed by the Secretary of the
Treasury, as will give opportunity to the citizens of the
United States to participate in the subscriptions to such
loan, and in allotting such bonds the several subscriptions
of individuals shall be first accepted, and the subscriptions
for the lowest amounts shall be first allotted." Before the
bill was finally passed offers had been made by various
banking houses to take the whole issue at a slight premium.
Both Congress and the Administration, however, favored
the experiment of interesting a large number of small
property-owners in the loan, even at a loss to government.
It was thought that such a measure would strengthen the
national credit by giving expression to the faith of our own
people in the integrity of the government. Other considerations of a political character also entered in, but with them
we are not concerned. As a financial measure for the
strengthening and support of the public credit it proved a
phenomenal success.

The bonds were issued in denominations as low as $20.
Subscriptions were received through the post-office, and
every *bona fide* subscription under $500 was immediately
accepted. More than half of the entire issue was taken by
230,000 of these small subscriptions, and no subscription of
more than $4,500 was accepted. In all 320,000 persons
offered or made subscriptions, and the total amount tendered
the government was $1,400,000,000. This rush for the new
bonds was not merely a matter of patriotism or sentiment.
During the progress of the subscriptions the price of the
bonds advanced first to 102 and finally to 105½. They now
stand at about 105. The lucky individuals whose subscriptions were accepted made from three per cent. to five per
cent. in a few days. The popularity of these bonds was
greatly enhanced by the standing offers obtained by
Secretary Gage from two syndicates to take the entire loan
or any part of it that was not covered by the popular
subscriptions.

This method of floating the loan will cost the government a considerable amount. In the first place it lost a possible premium. How much that premium would have been cannot be estimated because the bonds were sold in a broader market than would have otherwise existed. But it would have been at least two per cent., for even at a higher rate the bonds offer a favorable basis for national bank note circulation. That is, at least $4,000,000 was lost at the beginning. Then the cost of handling the loan, paying the interest, etc., is increased considerably by the small size of the bonds and the large number of holders. It is just as much trouble to pay the 15 cent coupon of a $20 bond as it is to pay the $75 coupon of a $10,000 bond. Yet in spite of all this, the placing of the $200,000,000 loan of 1898 was one of the most successful pieces of financiering ever accomplished by our government. It demonstrated the perfect solvency of the government; it gave us a financial prestige which went a long way toward hastening the end of the war; and it so strengthened our credit that, had the war unfortunately continued, we should have been able to obtain funds to almost any amount on the most favorable terms imaginable. With a three per cent. bond selling at 105 during the actual continuance of military operations, we can safely regard our credit as unimpaired.

The final test of the success of the financial administration of a war is the preservation of the public credit.

II.—THE NEW TAXES.

The United States government has never resorted to internal taxes, except to pay the expenses of war, and with the single exception of the Mexican War, we have waged no war without the use of internal taxes. The first system of "internal revenue taxes", as we have learned to call them, was arranged by Hamilton, 1791, in the face of the most bitter opposition. An excise was declared to be "the horror of all free states" and "hostile to the liberties of the people." On account of the general hostility to that form of taxation—a hostility which led to armed resistance in the "Whiskey Rebellion"—the law was but feebly enforced. It was dubbed by Jefferson an "infernal system," and finally came to an end in 1802. To meet the expenses of the war of 1812 Congress again, reluctantly, resorted to internal taxation, but the taxes then introduced were never satisfactory and were hastily abandoned in 1817. From that time to the outbreak of the civil war no internal taxes were levied for the support of the federal government.

The entire absence of any internal taxes and of any elastic element in the tax-system at the outbreak of the civil war added greatly to the difficulties involved in raising the revenues needed. Beginning in 1862, a vast and complex system of internal taxation was built up. Of this comprehensive system an acute French observer said: "the citizen of the union pays a tax every hour of the day, either directly or indirectly, for every act of life; on his personal and real property; on his receipts and in his expenses; on his business and on his pleasures."*

The heavy expenses of the war debt necessitated the retention of many of these taxes even after the close of the war. As the years passed by, however, the most burdensome ones were removed. Still a sufficient number of important internal revenue taxes were permanently retained to yield about $150,000,000 a year. The continuance of these taxes in time of peace, proved of great advantage when war broke out. That advantage was that they provided the administrative organization necessary for the collection of increased revenues. New taxes to be administered by the same machinery could be easily imposed and made remunerative within a very short time. Indeed there is almost no precedent in financial history for the immediate returns these new taxes yielded. The income from them during the very first month was over $12,000,000.

For the reasons explained in the last lecture it was

---

* E. Duvergier de Hauranne. *Revue de deux mondes*, August 15, 1865.

decided to raise the larger part of the revenue needed for
the war by enlarging the existing system of internal taxes.
The taxes of this kind in use were of three principal classes:
(1) the group on spirits, yielding, in 1897, $82,008,543,
(2) the group on tobacco, yielding $30,710,297, (3) the
group on fermented liquors, yielding $32,472,162. The
war revenue bill* doubled the rates in two of these groups
and rehabilitated a large number of the taxes used during
the civil war. The principles which guided the selection of
the different taxes were stated by Mr. Dingley when
explaining the bill to the House as follows:

"They (the Committee on Ways and Means) naturally have had
recourse to the legislation of the period of the civil war, when so large
an amount had to be raised, and they have found, after a careful consideration of the question of taxation, that on the whole it is better at
the present time, and we trust that that may be all that may be
necessary, that about $100,000,000 additional revenue should be raised,
and that entirely through internal revenue legislation. Hence the
war revenue bill which has been reported provides for internal
revenue taxes exclusively.

These taxes have been selected, first, because we have the machinery
for the collection of them now, and they can be collected with but
slight additions to the force and with but slight increase of expense.
We have selected them also because they were a source of revenue
successfully seized upon during the civil war, and because they are
taxes either upon articles of voluntary consumption or upon objects
where the tax will be paid by those who are ordinarily able to pay
them; and we have refrained from putting a tax in a direction where it
would be purely upon consumption, unless the consumption was of an
article of voluntary consumption, so that the consumer might regulate
his own tax, following what is the accepted rule of taxation in all
countries, with a view of imposing the least burden and disturbing the
business of the country as little as possible."

Briefly summarized the aim of the bill was to obtain the
money needed as quickly as possible. The question of the
equal distribution of the burden among the people was not

---

*Introduced in the House, April 25, 1898; passed April 29, by a vote of 181 to 131.
Reported by the Senate Finance Committee, much amended, May 12. Passed the
Senate, June 4, by a vote of 48 to 28. Conferees' report agreed to in the House, June
9, and in the Senate, June 10. Signed by the President, June 13. Went into effect the
next day, except where, in some cases, July 1 was specified.

raised. The revenue bill was strictly an emergency measure. Although the Senators showed a tendency to spin fine theories in regard to the operation of certain taxes, yet the equality of the system as a whole was not considered. Senator Allison said of it:

"In the first place, this bill is here only because the Government of the United States is involved in a war with a foreign country. If there were no war, there would be no necessity for this bill; and therefore it may be truly called, what it is denominated, a war measure."

It is not perhaps surprising, then, that the bill which was framed in this spirit contains a heterogeneous collection of taxes. It does not cull the fruit systematically from the orchard of industry, but plucks only a part of that which is most easily reached. The bill does not establish a system of taxation, but a group of taxes which absolutely defies classification.

We may study the war-revenue bill under the following divisions: (1) Taxes already in use, the rates of which have been raised. (2) New excise taxes. (3) New business and corporation taxes. (4) Transaction taxes and business taxes in the form of stamp taxes on business documents. (5) Miscellaneous taxes.

Of the three groups of internal taxes in use at the time the revenue bill was presented, one, namely, that consisting of taxes on spirits was left untouched. The rates imposed on the other two were doubled with the exception that the special taxes on dealers in beer and on brewers were left unchanged.*

The tax imposed on dealers in tobacco prior to 1890 was restored. The restoration of the tax on dealers in tobacco was regarded partly as a measure to enable the officers better to enforce the law in regard to the taxation of tobacco and cigars. No explanation was advanced during the discussion of the bill in Congress for not raising

---

*Tax on beer, ale, and porter, increased from $1 to $2 a barrel, discount seven and one-half per cent. Tax on tobacco and snuff, twelve cents a pound; cigars and cigarettes, over three pounds per 1000, $3.60 per 1000; of less weight, cigars, $1, cigarettes, $1.50.

the rates on spirits. Had that class of goods been treated as beer and tobacco were treated, no other taxes would have been necessary. With the improved methods of administration now in use there could be no reason to fear the wholesale evasions which vitiated the attempt to levy high rates upon spirits during the civil war. If, as was suggested in the last lecture, tea and coffee had both been made to contribute, and as now suggested, spirits had been treated as beer and tobacco were, we should have had ample revenues with the least possible additional cost. The amounts would have been:

Tea	$ 10,000,000
Coffee	70,000,000
Spirits	80,000,000
Beer	30,000,000
Tobacco	30,000,000
Total	$220,000,000

This is $70,000,000 more than the new taxes which were imposed yield, so that the additional rates need have been but two-thirds of the increase suggested. Indeed, an increase of half the amount suggested in the taxes on tea, coffees, spirits, beer, and tobacco would have furnished over $100,000,000, or more than the amount which the House Committee on Ways and Means thought necessary to raise by taxation. It is needless to say that such taxation would have been very much more easily borne by the people than the multitude of new taxes imposed. Had that plan been followed there would have been few of us who would know by actual experience that we were paying the expenses of a war.

New excise taxes to be collected by the use of stamps were imposed on patent and proprietary medicines and toilet articles, on chewing gum, and on wine.*

---

* MEDICINES AND TOILET ARTICLES.

Retail Price of Packages.	Stamp.
1 to 5 cents	⅛ of 1 cent
5 to 10 cents	¼ of 1 cent
10 to 15 cents	⅜ of 1 cent
15 to 25 cents	½ of 1 cent
For each additional 25 cents	⅝ of 1 cent

Chewing gum, 4 cents for each package of not more than $1 in retail price and 4 cents for each additional $1 in retail price, or fraction thereof.

Wine, per bottle of one pint or less, 1 cent; per bottle of over one pint, 2 cents.

Little can be said in favor of these taxes; they strike a vast variety of different articles of consumption and their effect is anything but uniform. Consumption is a very poor basis for taxation. The rates are so moderate, however, that there is little temptation to shift the taxes and the articles taxed are in many instances monopoly products, the prices of which, it may be assumed, are already as high as they can be made without decreasing the sales. In some instances, therefore, these are not taxes on consumption but taxes on the profits of monopoly businesses. There has, indeed, been no general tendency to increase the prices of these articles. To be sure the imposition of the tax has checked the tendency to cut rates and to that extent may be said to have raised the prices of some articles widely regarded as necessities, but that effect will be only temporary. While, therefore, these new excise taxes have not added a very desirable element to our tax system, they are not seriously harmful.

The new business taxes are of two classes. The first are those laid on bankers, brokers, museums and concert halls, circuses and other public exhibitions, bowling-alleys and billiard and pool rooms.* The second are those on refiners of petroleum and sugar and on pipe line companies.

In the first of these classes the most serious difficulties that have arisen are clearly revealed in connection with the application of the law to foreign banks. The law makes no special provision for them and they do not come properly under the general provisions. Strictly speaking a branch of a foreign bank doing business in this country has no capital located here. Such banks would, therefore, pay but $50, the minimum tax which all bankers must pay. But as these houses often do a vast business such a tax would be obviously unfair. The law of 1864 which was partly copied in the new law was much more explicit. It provided a

---

* Bankers, $50 a year and $2 for each $1,000 over $25,000 of capital; brokers, $50; pawnbrokers and commercial brokers, $20; custom-house brokers, $10; theaters, etc., $100; circuses, $100 for each State in which they do business; bowling-alleys, etc., $5 for each alley or table.

method for determining the capital of branch banks. The total capital of the bank was to be apportioned among the different branches according to the amount of the business done by each. This method was applied to foreign banks. That old law, however, laid a tax on deposits, dividends, and profits as well as upon capital, so that the burden fell with greater equality upon all the banks. While the inequality of this tax is best revealed by the difficulty of applying the law to foreign banks, it also arises in every other case. The amount of capital used is never commensurate with the business done, nor with the ability of the bank to contribute. There are, for example, fifteen commercial banks in San Francisco. In one of these the capital is nineteen per cent. of the business being done, as measured by the total assets and liabilities; in another it is seventy-nine per cent. Although the total assets and liabilities are only an approximate measure of the bank's ability to pay, yet this comparison shows that the new tax is many times as heavy on the second bank as on the first. Generally speaking the smaller the bank the heavier this tax is likely to be. The same inequality pervades the other special business taxes. A small theater or a small circus pays the same tax as a large one. Probably some of the smaller ones will be driven out of business. Possibly, however, this is not a result to be deplored. This whole group of taxes seems to have been snatched indiscriminately from the system of internal taxes which were developed during the civil war. The old system was by no means a complete or a just one, and the scattered sections adopted in the new law form far less of a system.

The tax on refiners of petroleum or sugar and on pipe-line companies which was placed at one-quarter of one per cent. on the excess of gross receipts above $250,000 a year is the remnant of a tax on the gross receipts of nearly all corporations which was proposed by the majority of the Senate Committee on Finance. The Republican minority of that committee, however, objected to such a sweeping tax, first, on the ground that it would burden many commodities several times over, and second, on the ground that many corporations, and especially the smaller ones, had to compete with unincorporated business houses and firms, and that the latter would be given an advantage. It was urged during the discussion that the tendency to form corporations was a public calamity, and should be checked by this form of taxation. A tax on the gross receipts of railroads, bridges, canals, express companies, ferries, lotteries, ships, barges, stages, steamboats, and telegraph and insurance companies had been used with great success during the civil war. It was proposed to renew this tax and to extend it to all corporations in spite of the fact that many of them were heavily taxed by other parts of the law. There were very large elements of injustice in the proposed tax, and the only argument advanced in favor of retaining the tax on the oil and sugar trust was that they were monopolies. The tax is not severe. It will not be above one and one-quarter cents per hundred pounds of sugar nor above one and one-half cents per hundred gallons of oil at the prevailing wholesale rates, so that there will be little temptation to shift the tax even if the companies would not lose more by reduced sales from an attempt to raise prices than they would gain by shifting the tax. There is little likelihood that the tax will affect retail prices.

A very large number of transaction taxes and of business taxes was levied in the form of stamp taxes on business documents and on the means of communication. These taxes are usually known as stamp taxes, but the name indicates merely the means of collection and shows nothing of the nature of the tax. In general these taxes are based upon a recognition of the fact that when wealth is transferred from one person to another its existence is manifested and a convenient moment occurs for the imposition of a tax. When such a transfer is accompanied by a document which is legal evidence of the title of the new owner it is easy for the government to refuse legal recognition to such a document unless accompanied by the evidence that the tax has been paid. It is, therefore, practically impossible to evade such a tax. The most convenient way of collecting these taxes is by the sale of stamps which are to be attached to the documents as evidence of payment. There are two features of these taxes which commend them as emergency taxes. In the first place, even at a low rate they can be made to yield a considerable income, and the return is a quick one, as large the first month as at any time afterward. In the second place they are very inexpensive to administer: the taxpayer himself acts as tax-collector and when he goes to the office to purchase the stamps brings in the revenue. He cannot omit to pay his tax lest his document prove illegal. During the civil war and for many years afterward stamp taxes of this sort were in use. Many of the provisions of the old law were transferred to the new law, and the changes and omissions are rarely for the better.

It would be tedious to enumerate all the transactions which are taxed in this way, nor is it necessary, as I can comment on but few of them. The first thing that strikes one who carefully scans the long schedules of these taxes is that they are frightfully unequal. Only here and there are they graded according to the value of the thing taxed. Thus the tax on the issue of corporation stocks is five cents on each $100 of the par value, and on the transfer of a stock is two cents on each $100 of the par value. But the par value of a stock is a perfectly arbitrary thing, a mere name. It is usually $100, but the true value may be anywhere from one cent to $1,000 or over, according to the success of the enterprise. So, too, with checks and drafts; whatever the value may be, the tax is always two cents. Indeed, in this particular case the form of the tax defeats its end as a revenue measure, for it has simply resulted in the writing of fewer and of larger checks, and more has been lost to the postal revenues through less frequent remittances than has been gained from the tax on checks.

All of that part of the law which deals with drafts and bills of exchange is so faultily drawn as to be practically unintelligible. The technical terms of banking are used in strange and unusual senses, and totally incongruous things, such, for example, as inland bills of exchange and certificates of deposit bearing interest are grouped together. These provisions should have been drawn by a practical banker. Had the new tax law not been supported by that patriotic sentiment which so largely aided its enforcement, this particular part of the law would have given rise to more law suits than revenue.

Included under the stamp taxes are certain taxes directed more or less vaguely at certain classes of corporations. These are the taxes on freight bills, express receipts, parlor and sleeping car tickets, telegrams and telephone messages, and passage tickets to foreign countries. The rates on the last are graded according to value, but on all the others are uniform at one cent each, except that no tax falls on telephone messages below fifteen cents. The tax on telephone messages is not collected by stamps. It is easy to see that this is a most unequal system. There has been much discussion as to whether it was the intention of the law that the stamp should be furnished by the companies or by their patrons. This is really a matter of little moment. In some cases the tax is so slight as to be entirely immaterial. In such cases the companies have furnished the stamps themselves to save their patrons any annoyance, and have not changed their rates. In other cases the tax is so severe that if the companies furnish the stamps they will be obliged to shift the tax by raising their rates, in order to live. If the tax were paid by the express companies it would vary from four per cent. of the gross receipts down to practically nothing. For doing a twenty-five-cent errand the express company would pay one cent, and no more for a shipment of $1,000,000 in gold. The express companies have asserted that if they have to pay the tax it will take half of their profits. The tax is also very severe on telegrams. The average telegram, it has been estimated, costs 24.3 cents and the average profit is six cents, of which the tax is 16⅔ per cent. Whatever may have been the intention of the law as to who should furnish the stamp in such cases, it is clear that the tax will be shifted to the patron of the company. If it is finally decided that the company must furnish the stamp, then the rates will have to be raised, and the patron will have to pay the tax just as much as if he furnished the stamp himself. Taxes which appropriate for the use of the government from ten per cent. to fifty per cent. of the net profits of any business are bound to be shifted. Still the companies cannot escape considerable loss even by shifting the tax. If they raise the rates in order to cover the tax their business will fall off, while the expense of doing it will not decrease in like measure. If they could raise their rates without loss of business there is every reason to suppose they would do so, tax or no tax. On the other hand the public is the loser as well as the companies. In the first place it is obliged to pay the tax, or at least a part of it, and in the second place it is obliged by the increased cost to curtail its use of the facilities which the companies furnish. When taxation approaches confiscation it strikes directly at the welfare of the whole people.

It is a curious commentary on the hasty character of this legislation that the tax on those corporations against which no little hostility was expressed in Congress should be only a quarter of one per cent. of the gross receipts; while on businesses against which nothing in particular was said the tax is nearly sixteen times as heavy, or nearly four per cent. of the gross receipts.

Among the miscellaneous taxes the most interesting is the inheritance tax. The House bill had proposed certain stamp taxes on probates of wills and letters of administration. This was rejected by the Senate Committee which substituted the tax that was finally adopted. Inheritance taxes have been growing in favor in this country, as indeed they have in all parts of the civilized world. During the last fifteen years they have been introduced in many of our States. The federal inheritance tax falls on legacies or successions of personal property only. It falls only on estates in which the personal property exceeds $10,000. The rate is progressive in two ways. It rises from three-quarters of one per cent. on direct heirs to five per cent. on distant relatives and strangers in blood, and these rates increase as the estates increase in size, from an addition of one-half on estates between $25,000 and $100,000, to three-fold for estates over $1,000,000. In the event of a legacy passing to a distant relative or to a stranger in blood, from an estate of over $1,000,000 in personal property, the rate is, therefore, fifteen per cent. The surviving husband or wife is exempt. A similar tax was used during the civil war, but the rates were not so sharply progressive.

The main justification of inheritance taxes is found in the sudden increase in the ability of the recipient to contribute. Theoretically there is no serious objection to the tax or to its rates and general arrangements; except that the rates should have varied with the size of the legacy rather than with the size of the estate. There is no good reason why a man who receives $1,000 from the $1,000,000 estate of some distant relative should pay $150 when the man who receives the same amount from the $10,000 estate of a similar distant relative or stranger should pay only $50. The size of the inheritance, not the size of the estate from which it comes, is the important thing. It is likely to prove very difficult to prevent evasions, especially as the tax falls solely on personal property; and the high rates offer a large reward for concealment. Our experience with the civil war inheritance tax is not reassuring in this respect; although the receipts from that tax did increase from only about four per cent. of what they should have been in 1866 to nearly fifty per cent. of what they should have been in 1870. It is so easy to conceal personal property that if persons are inclined to evade the tax they can do so. A minor objection to this tax and one that should be remedied at the next session of Congress is that no exemption is made in favor of legacies to benevolent or educational institutions, which as the law now stands must pay the highest rates. Another objection is that many of the states now levy inheritance taxes, and in many instances the double burden will be very severe.

There is one very interesting point which should be considered in connection with some of these taxes. In spite of the fact that most of them were chosen from the list of those taxes which had been used during the civil war period and that, in their older form, they had been passed upon by the Supreme Court, there is more than a doubt as to the constitutionality of some of them at the present time. All of the decisions which confirmed the constitutionality of the particular taxes in question rest upon the same ground as that which ratified the income tax of the civil war. But the ground for the whole series of these decisions has been entirely removed by the recent decision of the Supreme Court in regard to the validity of the income tax of 1894. Briefly stated, the previous decisions in regard to such taxes asserted that taxes on the ownership or the enjoyment of property were not direct taxes within the meaning of the constitution. But in the now famous case of Pollock *vs.* the Farmers' Loan and Trust Company, which turned upon the constitutionality of the income tax of 1894, the Supreme Court held that a tax "imposed merely because of ownership" was just as much a direct tax as one imposed on the property. In the light of this decision, if an income tax is a direct tax, then an inheritance or successions tax is a direct tax and as such is unconstitutional; so too is the tax on the capital of banks, and that on the gross receipts of oil and sugar refineries. It might be urged that the tax on bankers is akin to a license and, therefore, does not come under the decision in point. But the wording of the act does not countenance any such interpretation. According to the law it is the fact that the banker uses or employs a certain amount of capital that determines his tax. The rest of the special taxes, those on brokers, etc., are not on their property but on their business and do not come under this decision.

But there was another point decided in this same famous case, according to which these three taxes are unconstitutional, even if they are not direct taxes. It was held that, even if the income tax of 1894 was not a direct tax within the meaning of the constitution, it was still unconstitutional because it violated that section of the constitution which requires that "all Duties, Imposts, and Excises shall be uniform throughout the United States," because it did not fall equally upon all incomes. That is because a deduction of $4,000 was allowed to be made from some incomes and not from others. If the income tax of 1894 was not uniform, what is to be said of the new inheritance tax, · which exempts all successions from estates below $10,000 and whose rates vary from three-quarters of one per cent. to fifteen per cent. upon exactly the same amounts of property? If the income tax of 1894 was unconstitutional because it did not allow corporations to make the same deduction that was allowed to individuals, what is the character of a tax which is many times as heavy on one bank as on another, or of a tax on one small group of corporations which lets all others go free? There was no attempt or intention to make these taxes uniform; and if the interpretation given to that term in the recent income tax decision is to hold, these taxes are unconstitutional. That decision was far more sweeping in its limitation of the power of Congress to lay taxes than any other that has been handed down during the century. By disregarding the long recognised principle of *stare decisis* in regard to the income tax the court overthrew almost every precedent in regard to taxation by which Congress has been guided. It seems, however, much more probable that the old principles will be reasserted and the decision regarding the income tax reversed than that these taxes will be declared unconstitutional.

Among the miscellaneous taxes there was also inserted one upon mixed or adulterated flour. The imposition of this tax is not mainly for revenue. It is for the purpose of regulation and to protect the public from unknowingly using inferior flour. On oleomargarine there is a similar tax that has been in use for some time. It was asserted in Congress that as much as seventy-five or eighty per cent. of all flour sold is adulterated by the use of ground clay, ground rock, "mineraline," or corn flour bleached by sulphuric acid. It is not claimed that all of the articles used for the adulteration of flour are injurious to health, but some of them are, and none of them has the same value for nutrition as wheat flour. The law requires these flours to be properly labeled and by imposing a stamp tax on them the government can enforce this regulation. Without such a tax the federal government would not be competent to invade this sphere of state activities. A number of penalties are imposed for failure to comply with all the regulations. From now on it will be dangerous for any person to sell mixed flour under the guise of pure flour.

The general system of taxation imposed by this law is not particularly burdensome as a whole. In some instances individual parts of the system run very close to confiscation, and the system is frightfully unequal. At the same time most of the unequal taxes can be wholly or partly shifted and the severity of the burden is thus lightened by diffusion. The inequality and injustice of the system which we have noted all through the law is, perhaps, a necessary feature of any system that is adopted in an emergency, when the time is lacking for the full discussion of a logical and just system. It emphasises the necessity, so often referred to, of arranging in time of peace a just and equitable system which can be readily expanded in time of war. During a war no nation can afford the luxury of tax reform for reform's sake. That is an enjoyment which belongs to times of peace.

Considerable comment has been made upon the fact that the bill inaugurated new taxes and opened new resources but left many better sources of revenue untouched. As has been suggested in this lecture, it would have been possible without the inauguration of a single new tax to raise all of the revenue needed. But whether this were by design or by accident it is strictly in accord with the best policy for the financial management of a war. In the first place, as a political measure, it is justified because it brings the cost of war very forcibly to the attention of the people. But in accordance with the principles outlined in the first lecture it is of the utmost importance that the war financier should not exhaust his resources at an early date. All along through the early stages of the war his aim should be to multiply resources and to preserve some large ones for the later and more desperate stages of the conflict should they arrive. Thus it is wiser to initiate new taxes at the commencement of the war, which will grow more and more productive as time goes on than to draw too heavily upon the resources afforded by the existing system of taxation unless that system is fairly comprehensive and equitable. As the war proceeds it becomes more and more difficult to establish new taxes and their yield is then often dubious. Unless new resources are opened at an early date they may never be available. Then again, the main purpose of taxation in time of war is to sustain the nation's credit. The provision, by new taxes, of revenues for conducting the war is of secondary importance. Much strength comes to a nation's credit from the reservation of obvious sources of revenue for future uses. In spite of the many faults of the tax system imposed by the new law when viewed by itself, we must admit that as a war-revenue measure it was a brilliant success. It will be judged in no other light if it is promptly abolished at the end of the war.

III.—READJUSTMENT OF THE REVENUES.

Although the war is over we cannot yet count the cost. Many of the war expenses still continue. Some of the troops have been discharged, but large numbers are still in the ranks. The territories we have conquered must, for the present at least, be garrisoned. These garrisons must be maintained until a final settlement is reached and perhaps for a long time thereafter. Even after the terms of peace are finally settled there will be many expenses due to the war, such as those connected with the return of the troops to their homes. It is highly probable that the new territories we have acquired will be a source of expense for many years to come. An "imperial policy" demands imperial revenues.

Our federal system of taxation has for years been falling into disorder and will not readily respond to new demands. The war and its consequences will but hasten the development of changes that were inevitable. When Congress meets in December our finances must be rearranged on an entirely new basis. Our new peace revenues must be larger than those we had before the war. Judging from the present temper of the country, we shall have a vastly larger army and navy, both for the home service and for our colonies. Eventually Cuba, Porto Rico, and the Philippines may be able to furnish a considerable part, if not all, of the revenues needed to support the government there. But for the present, at least, that is impossible. In addition to the expenses connected with the enlargement of our army and navy and the government of our new possessions there will undoubtedly be many new expenses incidental to the change in our policy. There is already a strong demand for government aid in the construction of the Nicaraguan Canal. Probably there will also be demands for subsidies for the construction of a Pacific cable, and for shipping to follow the flag into new commercial fields.

Many estimates have been made of the probable increase in the demands upon the Treasury after the war. There is no safe ground for such estimates and they are most of them utterly worthless. But although we cannot at the present time tell anything definite about the amount of the probable increase in our needs, yet it is obvious that our old peace revenues will not be sufficient. That means that the new taxes must be continued or some others substituted for them which will add to the revenues we have been receiving in the past. How the increased revenues will be obtained becomes, therefore, a question of much importance.

In the first place, the principles governing the *fiscus* during a war are, as has been shown in the other lectures, very different from those which guide it during peace. It is practically impossible to run along under the present arrangements. Our new taxes are unequal and crude. They were adopted in an emergency. Better and far more available resources were left untouched. The main object of the financier during a war is to preserve the nation's credit, and to that end he should reserve some of his best resources for the time of greatest stress. Consequently the first emergency taxes are not apt to be well distributed. Fortunately in the present case the time of greatest stress, for which, as we have seen, such careful preparation was made, never came. But one advantageous result of the ample provision made is that we are now in a position to deliberate properly on the new system which is to be adopted. We have funds enough on hand to carry us safely and comfortably over the intervening period. If the estimate made in the first of these lectures is approximately correct, there will be a surplus fund of about $100,000,000 with which to wind up the expenses of the war and to start on the new regime. With this ample surplus we should be able to afford the luxury of a thorough tax reform.

Winding up the expenses of a war is not an easy process. Ordinarily government accounts are so carefully kept and every receipt and expenditure so carefully checked that the exact condition of each department can at any time be accurately stated. But at the close of a war this model condition is not found. During the progress of a war the public accounts usually become badly involved. Thousands of men have been granted the power to spend public moneys. This spending is often done under circumstances which do not admit of strict control. "Red-tape" must be cut, not unwound. The commissary in the field must get supplies as best he can. Unaudited and unsettled claims accumulate, which cannot be investigated until some time after peace has been declared. Indeed, there are many claims that do not reach the Treasury for a long time. At the close of the civil war there were claims of this character amounting in March, 1865, to about $285,000,000. Most of these claims bear interest at a high rate and must in consequence be adjusted as soon as possible. The very first care of the financier at the close of the war is the adjustment of these unsettled claims.

The next step is, in most cases, the conversion of the public debt. War usually weakens public credit and the borrowing that goes on is not often on the most favorable terms. After the war and with better credit it is usually possible to reduce the interest charges. For the reasons already explained our credit was not in the least affected during the late war, and as the war was of short duration there are no debts that need adjustment or admit of conversion. Fortunately, therefore, this step does not ueed consideration.

These two things attended to, it is possible to devote proper attention to the removal, reduction, or readjustment of the war taxes. In the present case, for the reasons just stated, we cannot hope for much decrease in the sums required by the government. Readjustment rather than reduction is required. The new taxes imposed for the support of the war are not upon sources that can long be drawn upon without far-reaching changes in our industrial and economic conditions. · The public revenues are simply a certain part of the wealth produced by the people, drawn off by common consent to be devoted to the accomplishment of certain common ends. If more is drawn from the wealth produced by any given industry than is drawn from the others, that industry tends to decline, and if the burden is very severe the industry finally passes away entirely. History is replete with instances in which whole classes of the population have been ground down by unjust taxation, until they either disappeared as a class or saved themselves only by revolution. Taxes need not be severe or the amount raised excessive to establish a tendency which will eventually bring about this result. They need only to be unequal. One of the most potent causes of the failure of agriculture to advance in this country as other industries have advanced, and one of the most obvious causes of the depopulation of the rural districts is unjust and unequal taxation. The taxes paid by our farmers are not very severe judged by the standards of some other countries, but so long as the farmer has to pay double the taxes paid by other classes of the population the agricultural industries of the country will not thrive.

There is a comforting but superficial doctrine held by many people in this country which is denied by the plainest teachings of financial history. It is known as the diffusion theory of taxation. It has even been laid down as a general principle that "taxes equate and diffuse themselves, and if levied with certainty and uniformity they will, by a diffusion and repercussion, reach and burden all property with unerring certainty and equality. All taxation ultimately and necessarily falls on consumption."*

Such a theory as this may do to blunt the conscience of a legislator who is too busy "keeping solid with his constituency" to devote much attention to the bill to provide revenue for the support of the government. But it provides little consolation to those who cannot

---

* David A. Wells, in the article on Taxation in Lalor's Cyclopedia of Political Science.

keep up in the race with their competitors because they are obliged to carry more than their share of the burden of supporting those institutions which are established for the benefit of all. If the tax on banking makes that business relatively less profitable than some others, capital will inevitably be withdrawn from banking and directed into other channels. This process will proceed until the supply of capital invested in banking has decreased, as compared with the demand, sufficiently to enable a higher profit to be commanded by that which remains. So far as the capital remaining in this business is concerned the tax has been shifted. But the business community which now pays the tax is also deprived of its accustomed banking facilities and is obliged to get along with less than is desirable.

The principle involved here is very simple. It applies to every tax which is not general in its application but which falls upon one or two industries only. It is reasonable to suppose that every producer or seller is now getting the highest price he possibly can for his wares, or at all events is charging that price which in the long run will yield him the largest possible profits. If a tax is imposed upon one commodity while others are free, the present producers of that commodity cannot get a higher price merely because they wish to reimburse themselves for the new expenses in the form of a tax. The mere imposition of a tax on this one commodity does not increase the demand for it and only as certain producers withdraw from the business and thus decrease the supply do prices rise. If the tax is shifted in the form of higher prices by those who remain in the business, it is because the production of the commodity in question has been curtailed. Those who remain in the industry get the average rate of profits. But there has been a more or less important transfer of capital and labor to other lines. The community is not altogether so well off, because it is obliged to get along with less of the commodity in question than it has been accustomed to. The enjoyments, or the well-being of

society, are thus curtailed, and society has to console itself
with other things which are less satisfactory. Capital has
been directed into channels not ordinarily so profitable
which, consequently, are not so valuable to the community. Then, again, among the consumers to whom the
tax is thus partly or wholly shifted there is the greatest
variety in ability to contribute to the support of the
government. The tax is, therefore, still very unfair. Expenditure is of all bases for taxation the least equitable.
Who finally bears the tax is of no immediate concern here.
What we need to remember is simply that unequal taxation
changes the course of industry, diverting it from old channels and directing it into new ones, which are usually less
advantageous, because heretofore less successful and conspicuous. And when taxation is directed partly by jealousy
and envy of business success and is placed upon those
enterprises which have made themselves conspicuous by
their success, it directs industry from those lines in which
success has proved the necessity of enterprise and capital
and drives it into lines in which it is bound to be less
advantageous to the community.

As was shown in the last lectures, the new war taxes fall
very unequally upon different industries, and will in many
instances have to be shifted to the consumers, if the taxed
industries are to live at all. And we now see that the very
process of shifting drives capital and industry into new and
less advantageous channels. The conclusion is obvious.
We cannot and should not attempt to continue our present
taxes longer than is absolutely necessary. The retention
of these taxes merely because they yield the additional
revenue needed is anything but wise. A new system, just
and equal in its operation, is absolutely necessary.

It is a curious historical accident that our federal
government has never, until the present time, been obliged
to consider seriously what constitutes justice and equality
in taxation. From the beginning the tariff has been the
leading feature in our national finances. At first resorted

to in an emergency as a revenue measure, it has been maintained ever since for political reasons. Except under stress of war, or to meet the expenses occasioned by war, we have had an income sufficient to meet all our needs from the incidental revenues yielded by a measure intended primarily to encourage home industries by the restriction of importations and of foreign competition. There have been but five years in our entire history in which the internal revenues exceeded the customs revenue and those five years were 1864 to 1868. Since the main portion of our revenue system has been dictated more by political than by financial reasons and purposes we have not gathered any useful precedents which can guide in the reform necessary. The problem to be solved has never presented itself to our statesmen before this in any form. At the close of the war of 1812, we entered finally upon the protective policy which with scarcely an interruption has dominated our finances ever since; at the close of the civil war we were called upon to reduce our revenues by the removal of the larger part of that heterogeneous mass of incongruous taxes which had been levied for war purposes. At the close of the Spanish war we have a similar jumble of unjust taxes, which we adopted in an emergency and which have served their turn; but otherwise the conditions confronting us are entirely new. After the war of 1812 the newly espoused protective system promised to afford sufficient revenue to meet the increased expenditures. In 1866 we were receiving revenues far in excess of possible needs and the problem, although complicated by other factors, was mainly one of reduction. But in 1898 we have a wretched *extempore* system of internal taxation, one of the many heritages of our lack of preparation for war, and yet we cannot dispense with the revenues these taxes yield.. The question is, therefore, purely one of tax reform; and one which must be settled, so far at least as the internal taxes are concerned, solely by financial considerations.

There are still other reasons why the government should

turn its attention seriously to the problem of creating a new and just system of taxation. The revenue-yielding power of the tariff has been for years declining. Whether by reason of the protection afforded by the tariff or because of their own natural strength domestic manufactures have so increased that foreign supplies are less necessary. In 1897 the government received less than $6,600,000 from iron imports valued at about $16,600,000, while in 1888 the customs revenue from iron was $20,600,000 and the imports which paid these duties were valued at $50,600,000. This is, perhaps, the most striking example, but the same tendency can be observed very clearly in other cases. The decay of the tariff will be hastened by the new policy. For a considerable part of the dutiable imports which really afford a revenue comes from our newly acquired colonies, if they may be so regarded. From 1892 to 1894 the imports from these sources amounted to ten per cent. of our total imports. But the revenues which these imports yield constitute a far larger percentage of all the revenues, because they include some of the best revenue-yielding articles, such as sugar, tobacco, and hemp. If these imports are all to be admitted free of duty there will be a large decrease in our customs revenues. It has been estimated that five-eighths of all the sugar imported into the United States in normal years comes from our new acquisitions. At the present rates this sugar imported would yield, perhaps, $50,000,000 a year in revenue. So that unless we continue to treat our colonies as foreign countries we shall not only incur increased expenses for their government but lose the large revenues now obtained from the duties on their products. Unless the tariff is revised from a fiscal rather than, as has been the case in the past, from a political point of view, it must inevitably surrender its place as the main source of revenue.

The principles according to which the new system of taxation should be arranged are simple and evident, but their application will be most difficult. Taxation should be in proportion to ability. Each man should contribute to

the common good according as he is able. If the burden
of taxation is evenly distributed so that each man's load is
proportioned to his strength, it is easily carried.

But in the application of these simple, self-evident
principles to the reform of federal taxation there are many
difficulties. In the first place the federal government is
debarred by an unfortunate interpretation of the constitution, from using that form of taxation, which should make
the backbone of any correct system. That is direct taxation. In the second place the maxim that taxation should
be in proportion to ability applies to the system as a whole,
to the totality of taxes paid by the citizen, and not to any
part by itself. The federal government is not the only
taxing authority in the land. There are also the States
and their different local divisons. There are few citizens
who do not pay taxes to at least four different authorities,
the federal, the state, the county, and the city or town
governments, and in some cases eight or more different
authorities may attack the same unfortunate individual
with their tax bills. To establish an equitable system
under such conditions requires a sharp definition of the
field of action for each different authority. Fortunately we
have such a division practically established by law and
custom. In a general way the States cannot levy indirect
taxes, nor the federal government direct taxes except by
apportionment, and that is so obviously and wickedly
unjust as to be excluded. It is foreign to my present
purpose to discuss the division of the field between the
State and its local divisions. But although the federal
government is confined to indirect taxes there is danger
that these taxes may draw from the same sources that the
state taxes draw from. The States may tax the property
or the income it yields directly and the federal government
may lay an indirect tax upon the same wealth in process of
transfer or acquisition.

A third group of difficulties besets the establishment of
a new and equitable system of taxation for the federal

government. These are political in character. A strong political party insists upon the continued recognition of the political features of the tariff. Protection must be maintained and any revision of the tariff for fiscal purposes must not interfere with that. It would be useless to discuss any plan which did not allow for this fact, and it is equally useless to discuss the advisability of protection, for that is now the settled policy. If for revenue purposes a tax is placed on the raw materials required in any protected industry compensatory duties must be added to the duties on the manufactured products. These difficulties are too familiar to need any explanation here. Other forces in the political field make for the use of the taxing power for purposes other than revenue. It is so easy to make political capital by placing destructive taxes on the "money power," on "Wall Street," on corporations and trusts, etc., that when it is proposed to make these elements bear their fair share of the burden of supporting the government under which they thrive, voices are sure to be heard demanding that the burden be greater on these than on any other elements. When behind this cry there is the threat of a new sectionalism, these voices become extremely powerful.

But this third group of difficulties is not new, nor is it peculiar to our own country or time, except in its specific manifestations. In all times and in all countries the power of taxation has been used by those politically strong to strengthen themselves and to oppress those politically weak. It would be unreasonable to expect that our own government would escape similar influences. Our government is too much of the people to be really for the people.

Such being some of the difficulties in the way of the realization of the ideal system, what plans are practically available? Among the most prominent plans presented in the last Congress was one for an income tax. This was rejected because it was felt to be impossible to frame an income tax law which would be constitutional in view of the recent decision of the Supreme Court in reference to the income tax law of 1894. Various plans were suggested for overcoming this adverse decision. Among other plans it was proposed that the Supreme Court should be "packed" to secure a reversal of the obnoxious opinion. This suggestion is revolting to every honest citizen, whatever view he may take of that decision. We have learned by the experience of a century that the Supreme Court always stands for the best good of all. The only proper way in which we can overcome the legal verdict of the Supreme Court is by a constitutional amendment. There is little doubt that an amendment intended to give the federal government the right to use any system of taxation that may seem advisable would be eagerly adopted.

But until such an amendment is adopted, it is useless to discuss a federal income tax. Moreover, it is quite possible to arrange a just and equitable system under the present distribution of powers, and it is at least a debatable question whether the income tax should not be reserved for the States, rather than be used by the federal government. At present, the taxes used by the majority of our States are frightfully unjust and oppressive, and the best substitute for them is an income tax. A fairly satisfactory system could be arranged consisting of indirect taxes for the federal government, income taxes for the States, and real property taxes for the local divisions. At all events this is the best solution possible under the present constitutional laws. The future development will undoubtedly require a different system and for that reason it is to be regretted that the taxing power of Congress is so limited. So long as the State governments continue an important part of our political system their financial support must be assured, and the form of taxation best adapted to their use is the income tax. An "imperial" policy will necessarily lead to greater centralization in our political system and gradually the functions of the States will be absorbed by the federal government. Indeed the movement in that direction was already clearly discernible even before the war. A uniform bankruptcy law is but the beginning of federal economic legislation. We already contemplate a uniform divorce law as a desirable probability. That is the beginning of federal social legislation. The federal government has already begun to regulate adulterated foods. With the increase in the federal military power the State militia sinks in importance. In short there is a decided tendency to diminish State activities. That the "imperialistic" movement will strengthen these tendencies goes without saying. The importance, therefore, of reserving the income tax for the use of the State governments decreases as the power and functions of the federal government increase.

Inasmuch, however, as we have a present problem to solve we must solve it in the light of the present powers of Congress. Viewed in this light there is but one course for Congress to pursue. That course consists in raising the the required revenues by the least objectionable indirect taxes. The selection of the articles to be taxed in this way so as to form a fairly just and equitable system is no easy matter. In order that the revenues obtained be sufficiently large the articles taxed must be of large consumption. In order that the expenses of collection be not unduly increased the number of articles taxed must not be great. But a tax on the articles consumed by the largest number of persons falls more heavily on the poor than on the rich. What the rich man spends on tea, coffee, sugar, tobacco, and beer is but a small fraction of his income. What the poor man spends on these is relatively a large part of his wages. The luxuries of the rich can be taxed to round out the system a little, but the taxation of luxuries is not productive of much revenue and the expenses of collection are relatively great.

In short, no system of indirect taxes arranged with a view to getting a satisfactory revenue can be altogether just and equitable in and of itself. It must be supplemented by other taxes. The taxes levied by the States and cities should, to make a well rounded system, be graduated so that the men who already contribute heavily according to their ability for the support of the federal government should have some relief from the other burdens.

The experience of all nations has shown that the closest approach to justice possible in the use of a system of indirect taxes consists in laying moderate taxes on such articles of wide consumption as salt, tea, coffee, sugar, and beer; heavier taxes on such luxuries as wines, liquors, tobacco, and silks. In this connection the actual systems of other countries are instructive. England has customs duties on spirits, beer, tea, tobacco, wine, coffee, and a few other articles; and excises mainly on spirits and beer. The articles in the French tariff which yield any considerable revenue are coffee, grain, sugar, petroleum, wine, and cocoa; the principal excises fall on wine, spirits, and tobacco. German excises fall on drinks, tobacco, and sugar; and her list of revenue-yielding customs duties is about the same as that of England with the addition of grain.

As was suggested in the last lecture, the United States could obtain ample additional revenue (retaining the protective system unaltered) by a slight increase over the old rates in the internal taxes on tobacco, spirits, and beer, and moderate taxes on coffee and tea imported. If to this list there be added taxes on wines and other luxuries, we should have a fairly satisfactory system without heavy rates on any one article. Summed up in a few words the conclusion is, that Congress should first abolish the unjust and unequal taxes imposed in an emergency by the war-revenue bill. Then as a second step, the tariff should be revised; not by juggling with the protective rates, which so long as they remain protective can never be made to yield any considerable revenue, but by adjusting the rates upon the revenue-yielding imports. There is nothing in this suggestion that should in any way rouse the opposition of either party. And lastly there should be established a system of excises or internal indirect taxes on those luxuries and comforts of universal consumption which the experience of nations has shown to be most productive of revenue. In short, the federal government should obtain its revenues from indirect taxes on articles of widest consumption and lay no taxes upon capital or upon industry.

It may be urged that such a system of federal taxes would not, considered by itself, lay sufficient burden upon men of wealth. But the federal system is only a part of our tax system and it is not the part in which the final adjustment of taxation to ability should take place. When properly supplemented by the State and local systems of taxation, these taxes will form a fairly complete system, which, while far from perfect, will be a great advance upon the present system.